Fabulous Beast

Fabulous Beast

Patricia Ace

FREIGHT BOOKS

First published in the UK March 2013
By Freight Books
49-53 Virginia Street
Glasgow, G1 1TS
www.freightbooks.co.uk

A CIP catalogue reference for this book is avail ble from the British
Library.

ISBN 978-1-908754-01-1

Typeset by Freight in Meta Serif

Printed and bound by Bell and Bain, Glasgow

the publisher acknowledges investment from
Creative Scotland toward the publication of this book

Acknowledgements

Acknowledgements are due to the editors of the following magazines and anthologies in which some of these poems, or other versions of them, first appeared:

Booklight (Knucker Press), *Chapman, New Writing Scotland 28*, Perth & Kinross Council poetry postcards, *The Journal, Northwords Now, Assent, The Sandhopper Lover & other stories and poems* (Cinnamon Press), *Poetry Scotland, Pushing Out the Boat, Gutter, 14, The Aesthetica Creative Works Annual, Mslexia, My Mother Threw Knives* (Second Light Publications), *Thin Bright Blade, Stone Tide* (Perth & Kinross Libraries), *Orbis, The North, The Rialto, Poetry News*.

Some of these poems appeared in the chapbook First Blood (HappenStance Press), 2006.
'Blood Nurse' *won First Prize in The Words Out! 2 Poetry Competition, 2003.*
'Ruby Turning Thirteen' *won Third Prize in Mslexia's Women's Poetry Competition, 2008.*
'Skye lines' *won First Prize in Aesthetica's Creative Works Competition (poetry section), 2008.*
'Gathering' *was Second Runner Up in The Gathering 2009 Poetry Competition.*
'Sixteen' *was featured in the touring exhibition Dualism: Portraits & Poems, 2010.*
'Papa Joe' *won First Prize in the Plough Poetry Prize (Open Category), 2011.*

Heartfelt thanks go to the late Philip Hobsbaum, Robert Alan Jamieson, Brian McCabe, Soutar House Writers, Hazel Buchan Cameron, Lilla Scott, Caroline Mackay, Helena Nelson, Tom Leonard, Michael Schmidt, Tessa Ransford, Linda Cracknell, Catherine Smith, Kona Macphee, Vicki Feaver, Gill Andrews, Stephanie Green and especially Jane McKie for her perceptive and sensitive editing.

To Carole Jean Ace and i.m. Alan George Ace

Contents

Skye lines

I

a stone – a rock
a single track

an aird – a stack
a dolphin's back

Hallaig – a cairn
a cataract

Sorley MacLean
into the main

II

a cliff – a drop
a long way down

a dun – a broch
a long road home

a fence – a gull
a scallop shell

a coral beach
a pilgrimage

a Cuillin view
a ringing rock

a scarp – a loch
a sunset too

III

harbour – heron
the *Bella Jane*

small lights in boats
jetty – a float

a castle – a keep
sheer drop – steep

a lover's leap
a fishing fleet

IV

a four-winged isle   Trotternish
a daffodil   a splash – a fish

burning heather   the weather, *the weather*
passing places   silence, spaces

a bridge – a sound   a wave – a shore
a tide – a tor   a harbinger

Settlement

The bright grasses nod and quiver.

Gulls like a line of stitching sewn
in the new-ploughed field. *The hands
that placed these stones one on top of other.*

Gargle of burn under culvert of stone.
Bog-cotton fairies drown in the marshland.
In the shady wood trees hiss their tales.

When the wind drops, I hear voices.

A lark flushed from her nest chatters, dives.
Sheep shelter in the lee of a bale.

*The people who settled here, faces
etched deep by distant lives,
scored by work and weather.*

The twisted silver stalks of heather.

Mating frogs at Loch Meallbrodden

On a sunny bank we found them;
hundreds of frogs, coaxed by warmth
from their winter homes,
croaking and basking in singles,
swimming piggy-backed in couples;
the reedy shallows a rolling boil
where they broke the surface for air.
Then groups of eight or nine together,
clumped in khaki knots,
one bloated female bearing several males
along her spotted back,
their bellies pale as the skin of a wrist.

From the wooden jetty we watched,
holding hands, frogs joining any other
that came in range, their frenzy so fierce
we turned and dropped our gaze and clasp,
watching our feet as we took up the path.

Walking by the hidden loch
that first warm day of sun, wasps clung
to nodding heads of bulbs,
hovered over beads of heather.
We passed the shoreline boathouse
slumping like a punctured lung,
crushed by months of snow and ice.

By the water's edge we squatted,
inspecting jellied dots abandoned there,
a thousand single eyes unblinking,
quivering in the blazing sun.

The women

Nudged awake from the slumber of nurture,
I find the women living in my house.

How they got here is anybody's guess; I'm sure
I asked for babies, but here they are anyway,

bragging that their breasts are bigger than mine,
filling my fridge with strong coffee and yoghurts.

Baby-gros and terry squares have given way
to sweaty gym kits, burlesque brassières;

skimpy pants curl on the line like tobacco leaves.
In school uniform they're more Britney than Bunty.

The women sit in my kitchen, eyes and thumbs
grafted to their oracles, giving an occasional grunt.

They know the answers to everything.
I wish they would learn to cook or drive.

They talk in their own language, as if someone
has pressed play and fast forward together,

their verbal salvoes punctuated by bouts of inexplicable
laughter every time I open my mouth to join in.

The women come and go as they please, like cats;
'Love you!' they call, jangling their keys.

In their absence the door of their room remains shut
and when I go in it smells of new shoes and musk.

Long-distance swimming
For Charlotte

Steam shrouds the surface like low cloud and wind off
the sea baulks at the pool's stonewall enclosure.
On the blood-red tongue and groove cubicle walls of
nineteen-thirties changing rooms, liver-spotted mirrors
express a preference for *Southalls Sanitary Towels*. Our
heads, calves and feet poke above and below stall doors like
a game of Consequences. Shared pasts sluice in the shower.
Vivid isosceles bunting sections the sky as I backstroke
energetically. You work on your front crawl.
Neither of us has mastered the breathing. I lick my

lips, tongue swollen with salt. Seagulls squall.
I ponder your work, my family, the gaps. How distant lives imply
division, difference. And yet we meet like this, resume,
our cycles still in sync, like women who share a home.

Aquanatal

We waddle from the showers to the brink,
assuming the grace of overfed swans,
expandable sheaths of maternity swimwear
bagging over ovoid abdomens, crinkled
as the skin of manatees. And Cheryl, nineteen,
the only one brave enough to wear a bikini,
a dark meridian arcing from navel to pubis,
like a line scorched by fire in a field of wheat.

We enter the pellucid blue, let go
the dragging weight from lumbar curves,
ankles puffy as proving dough, and float.
Our bellies and breasts break the surface –
icebergs or volcanoes with all their potential
for creation or catastrophe – archipelago of milk
and blood, cartilage, bone, tissue, ducts.
Nothing but the bubble and suck of our breath.

July 1969

My father takes small steps up the darkening lane,
leaving the light and smoke of the pub,
the shouts of his mates, for an empty house
and the smell of paint. The radio's crackling static.

On the bed a row of tiny clothes laid out,
my mother calls a *layette*. Sleepsuits, vests.
Tonight my mother sleeps somewhere else,
dreamless, heavy as a felled tree.

The first night since their marriage spent apart.
He halts between high hedges, listens to the rustle
of small warm mammals, breathes in honeysuckle.
He cannot understand how this day has come.

He will visit her in the morning, as Neil and Buzz
complete their translunar coast,
and tell her men have walked on the moon,
even bounced in the Sea of Tranquility.

He will visit her in the morning, stand sheepish
as she feeds me, not knowing where to look or
what to say as she slips her pinkie
in my mouth, burps me over her shoulder.

And then he'll drive her home to the little rented semi,
holding the wheel at ten to two, steady, for once
knowing where he's going; flecks of white emulsion
making constellations on his hands.

The best ten days of my mother's life

She didn't miss home or hanker after my father's company
or the care of my older brother, who on visits would cradle me
and call me a doll. And why would she? What need has a new mother
of anything but life's most pressing necessities? Food and water
and rest and every four hours the nurses carried me to her,
wrapped in a pink blanket, my fingers searching through holes
like seaweed caught in a net, and she would breathe
the brackish smell of my skull, marvel at the dark spot on my crown
pulsing like the center of anemones.

She read and ate and rested, watched the grey waves beat the shore,
slept away the crushing tiredness until, every four hours,
that tingle in her filling ducts, they carried me to her, tucked
neat as a gift in the blanket with the satin edge,
my starfish fingers opening and closing round flesh warm as water,
my cockle mouth locked to the rock of her breast.

An everyday act of genius

We have to do some tests, the nurse said,
prising her from the crib of my arms
where I rocked her and stared.
I studied every inch of her face,
locking into place each curve and dip,
the stove-in nose, parabola of cheek,
her wide-set eyes the shape of almonds;

as I would gaze at the face of a lover
or an icon, the face of my father
the last time I saw him, cast in death;
as if I held in my arms something precious
and priceless, the Turin shroud; the way
we search the clouds for something we know,
find there the face of an Einstein, a Shakespeare.

Love & drudgery

I get up, open curtains, put the wash on.
Make porridge, make tea, make toast,
feed the baby, feed the child, feed myself.
Take the child, brush her teeth, brush her hair,
find her glasses, clean her glasses, bathe the baby,
dress the baby, dress the child, dress myself.

Pick up baby, pick up toys, pick up tips
on perfect make-up from Fern and Philip.
Pick up the child from playgroup, feed the baby,
change the baby, hoover the carpet, plan the menu.
I make the tea, wipe the table, wipe the child,
hang the washing, cook the meal, wash the dishes,
scrub the floor, make the beds, brush the stairs,
put the child on the potty, fold the wash, put the
ironing in the oven.

I watch *Sesame Street* and find it entertaining.
I find glasses, wipe glasses, wash the sheets,
the bath mat, the child. I boil potatoes, baked beans,
wipe the menu, hoover the wash, hang the child,
fold the tea, cook the carpets, put the meal on the potty,
scrub the beds, burn the dishes, watch the washing...
beat the rugs, beat the child, boil the kettle, boil the baby,
I smash the dishes, rip the sheets, burn the pile
of tiny clothes that tower in the basket...
Burn you bastards, burn the basket in a great
big, bloody, beautiful bonfire!

I open the curtains, close the curtains,
open the curtains, close the curtains, open the curtains.

Fabulous beast

No, I'll not worship at the foot of this altar – the days
when it was nothing but rows and making up from rows,
heads locked in mortal struggle like two skinny strays
grappling in an alley over scraps the butcher throws,
panting under pressure, spines dipped then flexed
in a bid for the prize, each rib visible through pastry-thin
skin; heavy paws scuffing the dirt, thick-set necks.

No, make me instead a fabulous beast, something
lifted from the margins of a medieval text with the trunk
of a lion, part eagle, part dragon, shark-toothed and winged.
Make me change shape at will and reek of skunk.
Or failing that set me to slither in the dust, jaws unhinged,
my body shapeless and sassy and strong – yes, I'll swallow
you whole before I'll honour and obey, before I'll follow.

The Portuguese blanket

It kept us warm all winter as we lay
like two bulbs, our stems, our blooms
retracted back to a husk, dry, rough
as the patches of red winter skin which
crisp on our limbs in this harsh climate.

The Portuguese blanket. Bought as a last-
ditch souvenir of a holiday spent locked
in the love of three generations – my mother
and father, the girls, you and me in the middle
like filling, like superglue.

We paid for it with the last of our euros.
You wanted the one with the primary colours.
Something cheery, you said. King-size
and folded, it barely squeezed into the suitcase.
We should've bought an ashtray. Something portable.

I knelt on the floor, shoving it in. Still wet
in my swimsuit from that last dip in the pool.
You came up behind me, urgent, aroused.
Clawing down straps, pulling nylon aside.
Downstairs, our family piled in the airport taxi.

Ode to an avocado

Pear, let me sing praises to
the grocer's shelf where you doze
next your kind in serried rows,
nestled in purple cardboard,
like newborns in a hospital nursery,
waiting to be taken home, adored;
to your skin dark and lovely,
colour of wine bottles, covered
in goosebumps and yellow freckles.
How you fit,
cupped in my palm
as if made for it,
your Russian-doll shape,
both swollen and tapered.
The way your body gives
under my inquisitive fingers.
Your inoffensive smell,
greenery, cleanness.
Your umbilical scab
I can pick with my thumbnail,
how my knife glides through you
as through butter, through veal.
How you willingly separate
at the snick of my blade.
How the shades of your flesh
surprise me each time, bleeding
from apple green at the edges
through melon to lime.
The way your flesh turns brown
without dousing in lemon.

The concavity at your core, made
for the bite of vinaigrette.
How you wrinkle and furl against
the scrape of my spoon.
How you taste of nothing, then nuts.
How you slither on my tongue
like a sliver of soap, how I can't quite
grasp you but you slip down anyway.
How you never make me choke
or splutter but sometimes leave me
speechless. The unforgiving stone
lodged in your heart.

Button box

Some sewn onto ribbons,
teeny white and yellow moons
for a newborn's cardigan

or stapled to cards with names
like Fifties cinemas – Empire,
Vogue-Star, Excelsior: 1 /-

Here the brown velour
of a G-plan sofa; faux brass
from a blazer, ostentatious with lions.

Chubby criss-crossed leatherette
glossy as conkers, from coats;
six wooden toggles of a duffel.

A red flying saucer,
smooth as a discus,
launched from a late-Sixties shift.

All lost to the intimacies
of their old fabric habitats,
to the fingerprints, the sweat, the pulse.

The secret life of hair

Curled in the plughole a mesh of strands
fine and intact as a bird-nest lining.

Strung from damp black clothes on the pulley
catching the light, the long blonde question marks
of our uncertain line.

In corners and saucepans, perched on the rim
of a dinner plate, stuck to the screens
of monitors in static surrender, dangling.

On pillows, of course. Secreted deep
under duvets. Kept in a baby book,
ringed with ribbon. Locked in a locket
warm on a chain.

Twirled in your fingers, making you sleepy.
Pulled from a hedgehog hairbrush,
sugar-spun fish-net in the wicker bin.

Skin remembers

Skin remembers the time you slashed your face at four
falling headlong through that glass door
the press of wicker weave engraved on summer thighs
the soft place where that stray dog punctured your
surprised perfect flesh
skin remembers the slap your father gave in anger
skin remembers the wedding band's snug grip
the impression of the tangled sheet
the deep weal left by the edge of the belt

it remembers the times your belly swelled to hold
the growing life inside
tight as a drumskin, hard as an apple
remembers the surgeon's kind knife
slicing you free from your pain
the scar left behind like a grimace
the violent red worms fading to silver

but most of all it remembers
the crepe paper of your grandfather's hand
dry as the blown leaves that whirl in the yard
the tweed skirt scratching the backs of your legs
the kiss of the buttercup under your chin
the shame of the lie uncovered
the icy daggers skinny dipping in the black loch
holding the cat in your nakedness
the grey baby floundered on your belly like a salmon
the small warm imposters in the dawn bed
kissing the cold cheek in the hospital
the fevered tingle left by the first warm day

the quiet hunger of your children's father
finding yours while they slept
the hidden places where you carved away the pain
the wind stinging your cheeks when it ended
the places he took you in the dead of the night
the first time

as if you could forget

Secret

I kept it hidden, of course, locked in the wardrobe
beside the mink coats and banned python shoes;
tinged with the stink of mothballs,
under the jangle of hangers.

Some things are best kept under wraps.

My lips sealed shut against it,
I forced its bilious rise down, down
to my belly where it feasted on soft red flesh,
festered in my gut, turning my breath foul.

Some things are best left unsaid.

But I didn't see it coming when my hair fell out.
I rubbed at my scalp as clumps dropped to the carpet;
I thought I could detect a whiff of sulphur
on my fingers, the tips dark and crinkled as walnuts.

Still, some things are best kept close to your chest.

Spate

So we went to the river in spate,
you and I and the child of our making.
She was nine and the only one.

We heard it before we saw it, a sound
like wind but the trees still as stone.
From the bridge a bottomless burn,
swollen, poured towards the Earn.

The water pushed onto the path.
Stay away from the edge! Don't go too close!
Knowing if she slipped she'd be lost.
Holding this thought like a millstone.

The kissing gate drowned, we climbed
a fence instead, amazed to find
a mangrove swamp where the heron
once stood; nettles and hogweed.

The straight trunks of birch quivered
like reeds. Deep inside,
my last chance of children
adrift in my delta, my dell.

You point at the bank cut back,
devoured by the river;
attrition you call it, this eating away,
this hunger.

The woods

I took her to the woods,
her small damp palm in mine.
I said I'd show her fox-cubs,
young ones curled like kittens.

She was standing at the bus stop.
Her jeans skimmed her hips,
the ribbons from her ballet shoes
twisted through her fingers.

I'd seen her there before.
Thursdays she did dancing.
She looked like a dancer, skinny,
all limbs. Her stroppy little chin.

I coaxed her with a secret,
the fox-cubs in the woods.
She climbed in beside me, eager,
her breathing coming quicker.

I took her to the woods,
to a place I've been before.
Her crying got me going; her pulse
under my hand like a moth.

spring / everyday I wake to the massacre of birds

the white sun rises on silence   throws
its glare into uncurtained rooms

brown water waits in the barrow   slack
the trees in leaf arrested

the lawn heaves with spoils
sparrows   thrushes   starlings   swallows

the odd red breast   blue tail
sooty feathers settle as ashes in a grate

yellow beaks kindle   flecks of lava
their bones crunch underfoot

    *

today we woke to darkness
not knowing if we'd slept

the sky thick with gliding things
insects   flies of every kind

the air electric with hum and buzz
the black trees stripped of leaf and bud

The taxis descended at midnight

The taxis descended at midnight,
rumbled us through the city's
last breathing to a door
in a wall where life was.

The psychiatrist beside me
had regressed to childhood:
I'm frightened of the dark
he confessed. O, so am I.

Nerves

Is Mummy coming down today?
I asked Miss Jean as she flicked out the linen cloth,
smoothing it to the wood with hands warm from work.
No honey, I don't think so...Maybe tomorrow.
Has she got her nerves again?
Yep, she's about worn out with them. She frowned.
Now go and fetch me a flower for her tray.

Later, when I went upstairs for my nap,
I peeked round the door of her room.
Light glowed through yellow curtains, always drawn,
turning her world gold as Tutankhamen's tomb.
She was propped against pillows, pale as a bone,
and Miss Jean feeding her soup from a spoon
like they do to a baby who fails to thrive.

Coming home to mother

She lies on the lounger, watching
through half-closed eyes; skinny
in her red polka-dot bikini,
strings hitched on her hip bones
like washing line.

Sweat streaks her cheeks; grey trails
of mascara run down her face
like the leavings of snails,
coral lipstick jumps from her lips.
The white tips of a dozen half-smoked
menthols stubbed in an ashtray.

She stretches, yawns; her arm arches
for the glass on the un-mown lawn.
Oh there you are, honey she drawls. *I'm parched –*
fix me another drink, will ya?

Mum in old age

A Gordian knot, conundrum,
twisted double helix, monkey puzzle tree,
solved by a bold stroke.

Stubborn as an immovable stain,
fixed in language of her own invention,
halt as a rescue donkey.

A fridge-full of yellow stickers,
a lunchtime doze in the Parker Knoll,
glass of wine mid-morning.

A kitchen dinger on unruly pins,
top on inside out, incomparable moan,
Rumplestiltskin rum-punch-up.

The pop of a pill from a blister strip,
tick against the telly listings,
a deal or no deal.

The Birches

I find her in the garden, hunched on the bench
wearing the white nightdress, all collar and cuffs,
I gave her last Christmas. The red lunch-box clenched
close as a kitten that threatens to run off.
Hands sallow from the turmeric she's used to
dye her hair. I wrap her in the tartan rug
we always took on picnics. My *What have you
got there, Mum?* met only with a stare, a shrug.

I click the plastic clasp to see the things she
carries – pipe-cleaners, a bobbin, rusty bike bell,
a bookmark, a pebble, some foreign currency,
shocking pink lipstick, a battery, a shell.
Nothing of any use. These beloved things.
I hold her hand until it's time to go in.

Recovery pose
(After Spooning Couple, Ron Mueck)

Sometimes there is nothing more lonely
than to live together; to share the bed where
love was eager, every embrace a discovery,
each kiss, each touch, new-made,
the dunt in the wall in the shape of a heel,
a shudder which leaves a blushed face shining –
all shrunk to this silence, this stasis.

The grim fix of the mouth withholds its secrets.
I know this woman, whose empty arms press the sag
of her breasts, braced against the loss she enfolds.
His flesh curled like a fern at the back of her legs
tells her everything she needs to learn; nothing
is more lonely than going through the motions,
adopting the same poses.

Dido's marriage

coniugium uocat, hoc praetexit nomine culpam. (Aeneid, Book IV)

the nights I've wept alone
in the silent empty house

how love has come again
when I didn't know it could

you think you've lost some jewel
but it turns up in your sheets

    *

I could smell him in the gloom
as a bat senses predator or prey

feel his body warm as stone
heated by the sun all day

                                   a voice came out of blackness
                                   Is it you, my Queen?

                                   this man takes my hand
                                   holds it to his heart

                                   pulls me into darkness
                                   his tongue between my lips

                                   my thighs around his hips
                                   my nails on his spine

                                   the wind licking the cave mouth
                                   a tremolo of thunder

Sixteen

You weren't the best-looking boy at school,
not the brightest or the funniest or in the First Fifteen.
You hated cliques. I'm not sure I even remember your name,
although it could have been Alex. I remember plump lips,
and long lashes my friends would have killed for;
a shock of black hair, gelled and spiked.
And I remember that windy September afternoon
when we bunked off from Games and hid in the woods,
smoking and talking beneath the susurrus of turning leaves
until conversation lulled and you looked at me.
Roughly you pinned me against the trunk of the tree,
so close I could smell its sap, its bark biting my back
through my thin school blouse, streaking the white with green.
The surprise as your flesh sprang against my thigh,
your mouth covering mine as though saving my life.

Thistles for my dearie

He was the first to live I'd borne
he was my only laddie
the girls I liked them well enough
but he, he was my dearie

here's heart's ease for your ailing lung
here's flax-weed for safe passage

He sprouted like a sapling, strong
his body lean and leery
for he could hunt and he could run
so fleet, so quick, my dearie

here's barley for your aching bones
here's hawthorn for your splinter

The redcoats came when he was grown
and wooed him with their shilling
I blessed him with a grudging tongue
for he was young and willing

here's dove's foot for your belly's worms
here's primrose for your darkness

In desert lands he rose and shone
an ear of corn, my laddie
a stalk of corn they scythed him down
beside the road, my dearie

here's ivy for your callow luck
here's roses for your choler

And now my laddie's dead and gone
no more to run beside me
in desert lands he lies alone
and I've grown old and weary

here's poppies for your watchful night
here's thistles for my dearie

She comes back

She comes back to me in the spring,
her mouth a purple gash, tongue
bitter with so much dominion.

She stays shut in her room
with her books, looks down
her horsey nose or throws tantrums
about the rules of the house.
She's grown used to having her way.

She won't even look at her father.
Worse, she's been starving herself;
her form whittled down to a splinter,
a thorn. Her skin the strange white
of fungi, the kind force-bred in sheds.
What have you been eating? I ask her.
Nothing, she says.

She glows dimly like a low-watt bulb.
Come into the garden, I coax,
setting her each day
like a pot-plant in the sun.
She doesn't notice the nesting doves,
bats clumped at the eaves
like huge dead leaves, the lawn
mullioned with budding narcissi.

Slowly, over summer,
she takes up walking again,
picking wildflowers in the fields,
seeing her old friends.
My fingers itch at the grain in my pockets.

By September her skin has turned dusky,
her hair lightened all the shades
of the rustling corn; her limbs
long and lean and strong once more.

My girl, she picks blackberries
under skies banked with cloud; gathers
baskets of apples in diminishing light.
On her last night, she sits on my lap;
her quick fingers fashion a dolly from corn.

She comes back to me in the spring
and after harvest, she returns to him.

Ruby in the thistledown

That walk at Balnagard, hot.
We took the wide forestry track

to the top of Castle Dow
(from the Gaelic for black)

looking to find half a dozen
weird cairns at the summit.

An unrelenting climb through
Scots pine, birch, hawthorn;

we overshot the turn,
circled back on ourselves, lost.

Then Ruby, bare-chested,
breeked in camouflage,

delirious in the thistle patch,
shouting out *It's snowing!*

A sheen of silky seed-heads
stuck to her sun-blushed skin,

she released fistfuls like balloons
up...   up...   up...

Ruby turning thirteen

She comes home from school smelling of rubbers
and Tippex and, faintly, of sweat.
She cradles her cat like a baby,
carries him around like a doll.
She slops milk into a glass, grabs a piece of bread.
She's in a play about the seven deadly sins.
I'm this girl who's dead full of herself – y'know, flirty...
I'm playing Lust.

She shoves a pink magazine in my face.
Who d' you think is the fittest out of these guys?
She flicks the pages, playing it cool.
Her belt spells ROCK in silver studs.
Cookie Monster grins, ironically, from her t-shirt.
A guinea pig fidgets in the pocket of her hoody.
I study Shane and Jesse, Justin and Johnny.
He is soooo fit, she says. *He's got a six-pack. Look.*

She pretends to be a dog, down on all fours,
tongue lolling out, hunting for hidden treats.
Good doggy I say, patting her head, playing the game.
(She wants a dog more than anything.)
She lies on my lap, pretends to be a baby.
Her braces knock against the lip of her sucky cup.
I'm not ready for a boyfriend yet, she tells me,
I'm playing the field.

Saying goodbye to my daughter at night

The sound down low, the impossible blue
of the Water Cube in Beijing filling the screen.

A young diver stands on the board,
toes spread wide, heels edged over the brink.
His ribcage billows out and in as he lifts
his arms into an arrowhead.

I take my daughter and hold her close,
hug her to me until I don't know where
my body ends and hers begins – as stream
joins river, river meets sea – until we are
back where we started; the aqueous cradle
I know neither of us can ever really leave.

Headlights send their beams across the ceiling.

Back in Beijing, the boy arcs through air,
spinning like a bobbin on a loom.
Slices the water with hardly a splash.

The second time

my daughter leaves home it is harder; knowing I will return
to find her towel, still damp, scrunched on the radiator,
a pair of pyjamas left tumbling, forgotten in the dryer;
her handwriting scrawled across last year's calendar,
the days leading to Christmas scored out with black crosses;
the piano still and silent as a sarcophagus.

I drive home from the airport with a stone
lodged in my throat, that ache in my tubes again.
Back home, back to the new dog we've adopted to replace her
with its gorgeous face and high-pitched bark. Back to the black dog
who trails me like a ghost, tail curled into a bass clef;
who lies in my lap like a newborn, who cries for us all in the night.

Laptop

We haven't seen her since Christmas Day.
When she used to be everywhere –
sprawled in the living room watching TV,
rooting for snacks in the kitchen units,
hogging the PC in the study –
now she's confined to her room
like a convalescent, a Victorian child with some
dire disease; quarantined by technology.

From behind the door of fitties –
shirtless teens découpaged from magazines,
chiselled chests, waxed pecs, bleached teeth –
come blasts of repetitive pop,
the light hail of nails bouncing across keys.
Bedtime has lapsed by an hour.
Suddenly there's a distant boyfriend,
a friend of a friend found on Facebook.

I knock first and enter,
rounding up cereal bowls, sticky mugs,
scooping water bottles out from under the bed
where they drift with an absence of messages.
She lies propped against pillows,
wreathed in the blue of the screen.
I lean in to switch her off, my spectral girl,
alien creature, plunging the room into darkness.

Storm damage
(On Remembrance Day)

Strung out as we trail up Scolty Hill,
the spaces between us widen, gape.

My mother-in-law with her dicky hip
urges me to join her son up ahead.

Our paths meet for a moment,
then he pushes on.

Will you not walk out with me?
My fantasies keep me company.

The children forge onwards
into their certain futures.

Waterboatmen

The waterboatmen drift on the pond
skimming the meniscus on syringe limbs.
We sit side by side in silence, balanced
in the garden made of your mother's grief.

Blood nurse

Glorified mosquito, that's me.
The first point of enquiry
in a process of elimination,
looking for negatives.

I can raise a vein
to within an inch of its life
in a matter of minutes;
tighten the tourniquet

to its optimum pressure,
coax the baby-soft crease
at the inner elbow, reveal
the turquoise rivulets beneath.

Here comes a fat one,
pulsing under my thumb like a well-fed snake.
Small prick now, I warn them, casually,
sliding the steel into the lumen.

Quite often there's a noise, a spurt, a gurgle,
a trickle as it seeps into the vial,
the purple oracle. I watch for signs of fainting,
bleached faces, loss of speech.

All done! I smile and press at the pinhole,
bagging the labelled vessel for the lab.
I never learn the outcomes of my letting...
anaemia, HIV, leukaemia, hepatitis B or C —

it's all there in the blood
if you care to find out.
Are you allergic to elastoplast?
Results in a week.

The speleologist

I've never been afraid of the dark
or small spaces. Between a rock
and a hard place holds no fear for me.
My mother was a firm believer
in swaddling, routine.
My birth had nearly killed her.
Untimely ripped, my mother quoted.
Out the sunroof, my father quipped.

As a boy I made a den in the coal shed.
I loved the smell of it – mineral, earthy.
A tang of iron, something I remembered
from burying my head in my mother's lap.
My Dad bought me a boiler suit, a head torch.
That boy'll be a miner, he smiled. *Or a bin man,*
said my mother, *Look at the state of him!*

In my teens I watched hours of films
about submarines. I spent a whole weekend
just going up and down in a lift.

At home I keep the curtains drawn
and the heating off, forget to fix the washer
on that dripping tap.

Stump Cross

I negotiate petrified
limestone channels
like something being passed,
a molecule of food,
an egg through a tube.

Alkali drops gaze
from the vault like fish-eyes,
cling to ridged icicles
the colour of bruises –
moss, ochre, bone, rust.

Here I see a serrated
sheep's jaw, there an elephant's
furrowed leg. Lace curtains,
snowdrift, batwings.

All life here by proxy
slowly forming drip by drip.
Antlers, sandcastles,
organ pipes, lips.

Elemental

At first you were air to me –
essential, invisible, blue.
A breeze blown through an open window,
riffling papers, lifting dust motes to spin
in sunlight like planets, racing.

Sometimes you were water to me –
necessary, untenable, clear.
A spring in the hills where a lone walker
pauses, parched, filling her tin cup
from the source of the river.

And then you were earth to me –
mineral, secretive, black.
Black as the seed bed where the spore
takes hold, splitting into growth;
black as the burial ground.

But mostly you were fire to me –
incendiary, untouchable, red.
Flames licking the stove where our words
turned to ashes. But oh they burned
brightly, my darling, and well.

Love in old age

She's always popping out to the shops,
seeking the choicest delicacies
to appease his latest craving for chilli,
pineapple or chops.

On bad days she takes him a tray,
stooped over its weight on the steep rake
of stairs, prays her weak back won't give way
before she can deliver his meal.

She raises his felled legs onto pillows,
lets the blood filter back to his brain.
He doesn't like a fuss, she says, fussing;
then waits for his breathing to shush.

She reaches for his hand in the night,
tucking his arm across her chest.
It's brought us much closer, she confides,
If we both go together we'll be blessed.

Home in old age

The planting in the garden looks monstrous;
trees and shrubs jostle for light in packed borders,
foliage creeps round the rough edges of paths
ruptured by frost. The once-neat lawn grows lush
and long, unchecked by mower or shears.
The rhubarb has bolted. A glut of plums rots
on the grass, bearing a black crust of flies.

The house itself is just the same, hasn't altered
in twenty years. The faded curtains, dated furniture,
still witness the chimes of the granddaughter
clock which watches the hall like a sentinel,
disappearing time in quarter-hourly tranches.
My old room a cave in slate-blues and greys,
the scarlet roof of the doll's house limed with stour.

The changes, though small, are dramatic.
Cartons of drugs dominate every surface,
there are biscuits in the bedroom, flecks of blood
on the sheets, an ominous bucket camped by the bed;
hillocks of pillows in unlikely places, syringes,
a clinging smell of antiseptic.
Talk of adjustable beds, clean diets, stairlifts.

Conservatory in old age

It was the space he'd always craved, something
to replace the worn-out lean-to that clung
to the outside wall like a glass eye; where his wife
fostered grape vines and cavies with forensic attention,
claiming *Everything grows with love.*

She took some convincing, resisting his entreaties
with the complaint of another room to clean,
where would the guinea pigs live and anyway
what about the upheaval, the expense?
But eventually both she and the lean-to caved in.

Once it was built, they couldn't get enough of it,
forsaking the front room and its twilit gloom
for basking in soporific warmth, the longed-for light
streaming from dawn to night. Winter blues banished,
she abandonned the lightbox he'd made her.

He ordered a telescope, more powerful binoculars,
decorated the eaves with elaborate feeders, fat balls,
kept a keen look-out for planets and cats.
She expanded her repetoire, adding black-eyed Susan,
red-plumed cacti, bougainvillaea – hot flashes of fuscia.

How things work

I always found you in the shed, penned in
by dark smells – creosote, sawdust and oil;
spread on the bench the parts of an engine
you were putting together, making it whole.

Dad, remember how the porcelain jug
slipped from my grasp at the tap, how I gulped
Can you fix it? from the clasp of your hug?
But some things, I learned, just cannot be helped.

Today I find you dozing in your chair,
the stiff bag of your heart hoarding each breath;
the innards of a clock splay on the floor,
How Things Work, the book which gave you faith,

lies open at your feet but yields no clue
to this repair. I wish I could fix you.

Diary in old age

New Year's a conspicuous absence,
a week of blank days stretch across two pages
before business kicks in on the 6th:
that week a new car you'll never really learn
how to drive, then a new PC *arrived at 5.00 pm*,
a tax return mailed, a Burns Night, a blood test.

February begins with a bad cold
and an ultrasound, ends with a 24-hour ECG.
In March AOL goes down for five days
caused by *faults on the line* at BT. A mouse
is trapped at the Bowling Club on the 17th,
Broadband installed, *myopathy confirmed*.

Cambridge win the Boat Race in April,
a horse called *Don't Push It* claims the National.
Phil Mickelson, 'devoted father, loving husband',
takes the Masters. Your wife's birthday is logged
with characteristic brevity, *CJA − 69*.
May brings a Blue Badge but little else of note.

The summer weeks appear a blank wilderness
as Mixed Pairs and Ties are deleted, cancelled.
By June, appointments with specialists
feature strongly; biopsies and bone marrow
extracted by Dr Hunter, Dr Soutar, Dr Gillmore.
Drugs are administered. Writing becomes spidery.

The pages are given over to recording treatments
and symptoms, spates of hiccoughs, poor sleep,
dizzy spells, faints. *Tired all day, shaky / unsteady*
noted in a poor hand. A spell of weakness
in August leads to several entries of *Bed all day.*
Orders for monitors, urinals, supports jotted down.

The last entry, September 2nd, the day of admission;
the time, the Consultant's last name: 12.45 Dunn.

Truth in old age

An hour ago,
after afternoon visiting,
the nurse took us aside,
told us if his kidneys
gave up, there wasn't
much more they could do
except *Make him comfortable.*

In an hour I will pare
a satsuma into segments
squeeze their juice
onto his tongue.
He will ask
What's going on in the world?
and I'll read to him
from the paper,
some silly story
about prize-winning marrows.
I will stroke his ochre arms,
his stubbled cheek,
hoping that it's enough.
He will look forward to
seeing us in the morning.
He will say that he's tired
and will soon be asleep.

In two hours everyone
who loves him will phone:
his son-in-law in Crieff,
his sister in South Wales,
his sister-in-law as she boards
the bus in Aberdeen, his son
booking flights from America.

In three hours I will sip
at hot, sweet tea
under fluorescent light
while strangers are kindly
but not kind enough.
I will bundle his things
into yellow plastic bags,
carry his glasses in my pocket.

House in old age

It started the week after he died, the wake interrupted
by a faulty alarm screeching through the house,
child in a tantrum, banging fists on the floor.
Within days all the clocks had forgotten the time.

Since then a non-stop flux of things breaking down:
replacements are sought for the collapsing side wall,
the back door rottened by the prevailing weather
but new things are never the same as before.

Twenty years of make-do and mend and the house
is feeling her age. Lightning-style cracks bisect the plaster,
rust spores in the plugholes of sinks. Tradesmen are called.
They fold their arms, suck their teeth, shake their heads.

Neighbours

Alert to the arrival of ambulance or hearse,
they appear clutching casseroles and condolence
at times of unexpected crisis – sudden loss,
marital breakdown, prolonged illness.

United by postcodes and drying greens,
power-cuts, stairwells and entry-phones,
they share hedges, driveways and tax bands,
the wax and wane of house prices.

Divided by bolting leylandii, cockerels,
dog waste and drum-kits, lawn-mowing at dawn,
the inadvertent toileting of capricious cats,
they watch over your comings and goings.

They know the state of your underwear,
the brick that guards your back-door key,
the undisclosed smoking taking place in the shed,
that your grown-up son is back, lodging upstairs.

We must have you over for a drink, they say
but then you don't see them for months.
Your key hangs untouched on a hook in their hall.
They have your number, but they don't know it by heart.

Starter home

It was a quiet house, familiar, subdued,
a place where nothing much changed;
where the same wooden jug sat squat
on the dresser, the receiver of the phone
lodged in its cream cradle like a femur.

Ideal it wasn't. It's chimneys teetered
in the merest waft, it's slippery stairs
creaked under the inhabitants' felt feet.
The bushes splodged at the front lacked
attention, eventually fading to smears.

But the family who lived there didn't care:
Mum serving up the same meal every day –
plastic bread and cheese, swiss roll for afters;
lifting the listless baby from its spot on
the mass-produced rug. The older children

pegged to their rocking horses, balancing
in perpetuity, lacking the agitation to stir.
In the absence of car or lawn, uninspired
by DIY, Dad spent most days 'at work'.
At night they stared at the same red-haired

girl chalking her noughts from the telly
or listened to static on the wireless;
watched the stopped clock until it was time
to lie in the dry bath fully-clothed or rest
on the thin yellow foam on their MDF beds.

Comme ci, comme ça

I didn't realise love would be this way:
I shop and cook and clean, you wash the car;
a list of chores and tasks dictate the day,
the yellow-feathered fridge our *aide-mémoire*.

I fill the diary, sipping *Pinot Noir*.
You empty bins, chop logs, write cheques to pay
the tax, insurance, lessons on guitar.
I didn't realise love would be this way.

You mow the lawn, change lightbulbs, keep at bay
the dry-rot taking hold in our *armoire*.
I feed the cat, book tickets for the play;
I shop and cook and clean, you fill the car.

You buy the Sunday papers from the Spar.
I iron your work shirts, smooth creases away.
You tackle DIY, your own *bête noire*;
a list of chores and tasks dictate the day.

I sometimes wonder what you'd have to say
if you found me cleaning windows in my bra
or hoovering the house – *déshabillé* –
the yellow-feathered fridge door cast ajar

and in my mouth the stub of a cigar
and even though it's quarter past midday
I've drunk six cans of cold Stella Artois
and polished off your favourite *crème brulée* –
sorry, darling – I didn't realise.

Born to be wild

I never strolled down Bridge Street at daybreak in June,
ball-gowned and barefoot, champagne souring my breath
or languished insomniac in the all-night library,
lost in translation: *De Rerum Natura*

but one midnight, driving home, I saw the clouds
shift from salmon, through emerald to lime,
an owl whooping *son* to the sky's *lumière.*

I never joined that fire-juggling troupe
or woke naked in Black Rock, Nevada, straddled a Harley
and rode pillion coast-to-coast
wrapped round a man I'd just met in a bar

but once I spent an hour watching a deer graze the lawn,
her head dropping and lifting in the dim pre-dawn,
as she stopped every so often to stare.

I never said I *do* to a man dressed as Elvis,
danced for twenty-four hours on the beach at Goa
out of my mind on slammers and skunk or
had sex on a plane, in a elevator, under water

but when I lay on the jetty, I heard the roar of the air
as the swan's wings gave it tongue,
the loch's slosh as the wind tried to catch it.

Gathering

I will lift up mine eyes unto the hills from whence
cometh my help. Psalm 121

Walking on the Knock, aware of my breath and every move I make,
I climb in the footsteps of many forebears – legs drumming atop
a thick crust of ice after the hardest winter anybody can remember.

My feet punch the white like pistons: the body responds – cogs
in a waterwheel; head spinning with oxygen.
My heart thumps in the rhythm of a bodhràn.

Sap rises through soles from its underground store, its vault,
feeds the glow in my belly like whisky.
                              The hills above Glenturret
picked out in snow against a sky blue as the hackle of a thistle.
The air sharp on my tongue, clean and clear as a dram of malt.

All this I carry like a creel from the shore, a stack of kindling
gathered from the wood, but suddenly light, light now,
the spring of heather under my step until I get to the top and I stop.

Cobble Haugh

The soil at the fence is thin and high,
a pilgrim's path, treacherous with nettles.
Dreadlocks of wool cling to the barbs.
Drumlins stretch out to the carse.

On the far side of the copper Pow,
Greenland geese nibble at stubble
beneath new-mattress clouds.
Buzzards circle and mew.

At the place where two waters meet
silt blooms in the peat-brown stream.
Feet release the scent of garlic; I walk
through a puddle the shape of lungs.

By Cobble Haugh the river bubbles in sun,
the water drinking its brilliance, its dazzle.

My husband attempts the impossible

Oh, they've got a death wish
says the farmer's wife
when he knocks at the steading door
to tell her a sheep has died.

She tells him how, on the lush lower slopes,
they don't know when to stop;
keep chewing the cud
until their bellies blow up;

the wet grass drenching their wool,
making them too heavy to lift
from where they lie in their rumination
until, in time, eyes glaze, legs stiffen.

Still, I watch him from the cottage door,
kneeling small and sodden in the dismal field,
trying to raise one to life.

O there is something greater

At the far end of Puddock Pond I crouch on a seat of rock, at my back
the tumbled dry-stone wall with all its cracks and crevices, its eyes,
     smiles
and grimaces, its tongues of silky moss, vivid as river-weed.

The air alive, charged with beating wings and leaves in breeze,
fish lipping still water, beetles crawling through parched grasses.
From a stand of silver birch comes sound of startled bird-call, then
     silence.

The place I've come to escape the dull suck of work done for money;
a cuckoo calls from the wood, *Cuckoo! Cuckoo!*, her thick-shelled egg
cooling in another's nest. Out of sight a rustle stirs the leafy ground.

The doe's head swings over the wall and we are eye to eye, a yard
     apart;
her iris, the colour of the river, reflects a dark planet back to my gaze.
She whispers, *O there is something greater. Relinquish the childish*
     heart.

Lions of Guia

I passed them each dawn on my way to buy bread,
the two circus lions pacing in tandem, their match-head
tails ticking the bars of their trailer, stick in a wheel.

I watched them fight over the one patch of shade,
brought them fish heads from the docks and saw
my shocked face mirrored in the beryls of their eyes.

I heard the tamer was an egomaniac drunk,
so I slipped out at night, slid the clasp from my hair
and shook like a virgin as the padlock sprung free.

I stroked their square heads, their flat noses,
lost my fingers in the shag of their manes.
Blunt tongues licked the salt from my arms.

I lay my spine against the heat of one's torso,
wore him all night like the coat of a chieftain,
slept long in the tang of his ferrous breath.

I woke before dawn to the chanting of slave songs,
coming like prayers from their cavernous mouths,
Sometimes I feel like a motherless child, a long way from home.

I led them on silver leashes through the suburbs,
watched them squat on the lawns of the bourgeoisie,
unleashed them to stalk rabbits in white fields of wheat.

Little Octopus

they called her, the eight limb splay
of her spidery form making her an Asian deity:
one arm for smiting
one arm for wealth
one for compassion
one for grasping whatever it was she could hold on to.

Like her homeland, one eye looked East, the other
squinted West, but neither gave the whole picture.
Goddess, Changeling, Miracle, Monster –
these were some of the names they called her.
Pulled in many directions, she ended up going nowhere.

Instead, kept to the house, she studied her mother,
watched her concoct poisons for the day the soldiers came:
a new babe tugging at one teat, her father at the other.
She considered the division of labour.
She needed to be loved.
She needed to be alone.

She gathered her saclike body, her recalcitrant members,
packed up her pillow, her skirts, ran away to the circus.
There she learned the art of pleasing a crowd.

She stood in a corner of the hall of mirrors,
splitting herself into infinity.

Papa Joe

He came once a month on Saturday afternoons,
riding into town on a wall-eyed mule called Cyclops,
bare heels scuffing the dust – man, he was tall;
tall and wiry, his hair all straggles, smelling of linseed
and paw-paw, his skin the colour of syrup.

We called him Papa Joe on account of his coat,
like the boy in the Bible, but stitched from many rags –
taffeta, chiffon, seersucker – whatever the ladies
of the parish could spare; we recognised curtains, tablecloths,
the Sunday dresses our sisters had grown out of.

In the shade of the flame tree us kids squatted down.
He charged a dollar for a story, fifty cents a song,
and man, he knew them all – Sinbad and Bluebeard,
the Lost City of Atlantis, How the Whale got his Throat.
The words were like food to him, or sunlight, or air.

Our mouths gaped like groupers as he worked the words
into a charm, his voice dark and sweet as molasses. Then
he'd spend an hour in the parlour with my maiden aunt,
the blinds down, sipping rum punches in the cool of her room.

She would wave him off at sunset, a sprig of bougainvillaea
tucked behind her ear.
                          On those nights she made Bentleys,
bought us roti and hops from the store; on those nights
she lit candles and swung her hips slow in the gloom.

the stars coming out

entre le chien et le loup, dusk
on the cusp of day and night
a gull squats on the cliff
a seal slips off the rocks

the stars coming out

the tide fades in, fades out
the horizon smudges
neither one thing nor the other
time to light the lights

the stars coming out

here they come
pinpricks in a lavender sky
caught in the net of smoke-drift
scrawling from chimneys

the stars coming out

wheel against the gable wall
haystacks hunkered down
shadow cast from resting plough
ladder with a broken rung

the stars coming out